Eat Nothing White Diet

A Beginner's Step-by-Step Guide with Recipes and a Meal Plan

mf

copyright © 2020 Tyler Spellmann

All rights reserved No part of this book may be reproduced, or stored in a retrieval system, or transmitted in any form or by any means, electronic, mechanical, photocopying, recording, or otherwise, without express written permission of the publisher.

Disclaimer

By reading this disclaimer, you are accepting the terms of the disclaimer in full. If you disagree with this disclaimer, please do not read the guide.

All of the content within this guide is provided for informational and educational purposes only, and should not be accepted as independent medical or other professional advice. The author is not a doctor, physician, nurse, mental health provider, or registered nutritionist/dietician. Therefore, using and reading this guide does not establish any form of a physician-patient relationship.

Always consult with a physician or another qualified health provider with any issues or questions you might have regarding any sort of medical condition. Do not ever disregard any qualified professional medical advice or delay seeking that advice because of anything you have read in this guide. The information in this guide is not intended to be any sort of medical advice and should not be used in lieu of any medical advice by a licensed and qualified medical professional.

The information in this guide has been compiled from a variety of known sources. However, the author cannot attest to or guarantee the accuracy of each source and thus should not be held liable for any errors or omissions.

You acknowledge that the publisher of this guide will not be held liable for any loss or damage of any kind incurred as a result of this guide or the reliance on any information provided within this guide. You acknowledge and agree that you assume all risk and responsibility for any action you undertake in response to the information in this guide.

Using this guide does not guarantee any particular result (e.g., weight loss or a cure). By reading this guide, you acknowledge that there are no guarantees to any specific outcome or results you can expect.

All product names, diet plans, or names used in this guide are for identification purposes only and are the property of their respective owners. The use of these names does not imply endorsement. All other trademarks cited herein are the property of their respective owners.

Where applicable, this guide is not intended to be a substitute for the original work of this diet plan and is, at most, a supplement to the original work for this diet plan and never a direct substitute. This guide is a personal expression of the facts of that diet plan.

Where applicable, persons shown in the cover images are stock photography models and the publisher has obtained the rights to use the images through license agreements with third-party stock image companies.

Table of Contents

Introduction — 7
What Is the Eat Nothing White Diet — 10
    Understanding the "White" in the Eat Nothing White Diet — 11
    Why These Foods Are Considered Unhealthy in Excess — 12
    Principles of the Diet — 13
    Benefits of this Diet — 15
    Disadvantages — 18
What Are the Things to Be Considered — 21
    Considerations — 21
5 Step-by-Step Guide on How to Start the 'Eat Nothing White' Diet — 25
    Step 1: Understand What 'White' Foods Are — 25
    Step 2: Clear Out Your Pantry — 26
    Step 3: Stock Up on Whole Food Alternatives — 27
    Step 4: Plan Your Meals — 28
    Step 5: Monitor Your Progress and Adjust Accordingly — 29
    Foods to Eat — 30
    Foods to Avoid — 32
The Eat Nothing White Diet Food Guide — 35
    Breakfast — 35
    Mid-Morning Snack — 36
    Lunch — 37
    Mid-Afternoon Snack — 38
    Supper — 38
Making Smarter Choices – Week 1 — 40
    What to Eat — 41
    No White Veggies Salad — 44
    Easy Garlic Broiled Chicken — 46
The Reinforcement Period – Week 2 — 48

What to Eat	49
The Maintenance Period – Week 3	**52**
Food Choices	52
Alternative Recipes	53
Green Salad	54
Rosemary Veggies - Roasted	55
Bonus Recipes	**57**
Salmon and Salad Mix	58
Homemade Mexican Bowl	60
Broccoli and Beans Soup	62
Beef Sirloin Tips in Pepper Sauce	64
Lemon-Ginger Chicken	66
Grilled Teriyaki Chicken	68
Peach Glazed Pork Chops	70
Ginger Chicken Kabobs	72
Conclusion	**74**
FAQs	**77**
References and Helpful Links	**80**

Introduction

Have you found yourself sifting through endless diet plans, each promising miraculous result but leaving you feeling overwhelmed and uncertain? The "Eat Nothing White" diet simplifies this process, focusing on eliminating white foods from your diet - think white sugar, white flour, and other processed foods that often contribute to weight gain and health issues. This approach is not just another fad diet; it's a sustainable shift towards mindful eating.

What makes this diet stand out is its simplicity and the tangible benefits you start noticing almost immediately. By cutting out white foods, you're steering clear of excess sugar and refined carbs, which are notorious for spiking your blood sugar and leading to energy crashes. Instead, you'll lean towards whole grains, fruits, vegetables, and lean proteins, which support sustained energy and satiety. It's not just about losing weight; it's about nurturing your body with the nutrients it needs to thrive.

Think of how refreshing it would be to feel more energetic throughout the day, to see improvements in your skin, and to enjoy a more stable mood without the ups and downs caused by a sugar-laden diet. Many who have adopted this way of eating report not only shedding excess pounds but also gaining a new lease on life. They find joy in creating meals that are not only nutritious but also delicious and fulfilling. The "Eat Nothing White" diet isn't a restrictive plan but a new perspective on food that celebrates natural, unprocessed ingredients.

In this guide, we will talk about the following:

- What is the Eat Nothing White Diet
- Understanding the "White" in the Eat Nothing White Diet
- Why These Foods Are Considered Unhealthy in Excess
- Principles, Benefits, and Potential Drawbacks of Eat Nothing White Diet
- What are the Things to be Considered
- 5 Step-by-step Guide on How to Get Started with This Diet
- Foods to Eat and to Avoid
- 3- Week in No Eat Nothing White Diet
- Sample Meal Plan and Recipes

By the end of this guide, you'll realize that making healthier food choices doesn't have to be complicated. In fact, it can be quite the opposite. Welcome to a way of eating that feels good and is good for you. You might just discover that the key to lasting health and happiness lies in the simplicity of eating foods as close to their natural state as possible. Join us as we explore the benefits, principles, and joy of following the "Eat Nothing White" diet.

What Is the Eat Nothing White Diet

The Eat Nothing White Diet focuses on cutting out all "white" foods, particularly refined and processed items like white rice, flour, and sugars, to combat obesity. These foods lack nutrients and are linked to weight gain, diabetes, and heart disease due to their high glycemic index, which causes blood sugar spikes. By eliminating these "bad carbs," which are often found in baked goods and sugary drinks—responsible for a significant portion of Americans' calorie intake—the diet aims to reduce overconsumption and promote weight loss.

The American Heart Association notes the average American's high sugar consumption contributes to empty calories and health risks. The diet advocates for whole, unprocessed foods that are more filling and nutritious, supporting both weight management and overall health. It encourages choosing low-starch vegetables and organic options over foods high in sugar and simple carbohydrates, which are less satisfying and can lead to overeating.

Following the US Dietary Guidelines on whole grains can also help in maintaining a balanced diet. The goal is to replace high-glucose white foods with healthier alternatives to lower the risk of diabetes and heart diseases.

Understanding the "White" in the Eat Nothing White Diet

The Eat Nothing White Diet zeroes in on a specific category of foods often referred to as "white" due to their color and processing level. This category predominantly includes:

- *Processed Sugars and Flours*: These are found in a vast array of products, from baked goods to packaged snacks. During processing, these foods are stripped of their natural fibers, vitamins, and minerals, leaving behind simple carbohydrates that offer quick energy but minimal nutritional value.
- *White Rice, White Bread, Pasta, and Other Refined Grains*: Similar to processed sugars and flours, these grains have been refined, removing the bran and germ, which contain the grain's fiber and nutrients. What remains is primarily the endosperm, which is high in starches and has a higher glycemic index.
- *Potatoes*: Although not processed to the same extent as flour and sugars, white potatoes have a high glycemic index, meaning they can cause a rapid spike in blood sugar levels.

- ***Some Dairy Products***: While not all dairy products are considered "bad" in the diet, those that are high in fat and lacking in nutritional value (such as certain cheeses and creams) fall into the avoidable category due to their potential impact on health when consumed in excess.

Why These Foods Are Considered Unhealthy in Excess

These foods are considered unhealthy when consumed in excess because they can lead to several health issues, including diabetes and heart diseases. Here are some reasons why:

1. ***High Glycemic Index***: Most white foods have a high glycemic index (GI), which means they lead to rapid spikes in blood sugar levels followed by a sharp decline. The fluctuations in blood sugar levels can result in energy dips and intense cravings. Over time, this rollercoaster may heighten the risk of insulin resistance and type 2 diabetes.
2. ***Low Nutritional Value***: The refining process strips away essential nutrients such as fiber, vitamins, and minerals. Consuming white foods therefore often means missing out on these important nutrients, which can negatively impact overall health, digestion, and even mental health.

3. ***Increased Risk of Weight Gain and Obesity***: Due to their high GI and low satiety index, white foods can lead to overeating and weight gain. The lack of fiber means these foods don't fill you up as much or for as long as their whole-grain or unrefined counterparts, leading to increased calorie consumption throughout the day.
4. ***Contribution to Heart Disease and Other Conditions***: Diets high in refined grains and sugars have been linked to a higher risk of heart disease, certain cancers, and other chronic conditions. This is partly due to the inflammatory response they can trigger in the body, along with their contribution to obesity and metabolic syndrome.

In summary, while white foods can fit into a healthy diet in small amounts, relying on them heavily can lead to health issues. The Eat Nothing White Diet encourages individuals to choose whole, unprocessed foods rich in nutrients to support overall health, stabilize blood sugar levels, and promote sustainable weight management.

Principles of the Diet

The "Eat Nothing White" diet is based on a concept aimed at improving health and facilitating weight loss by avoiding white-colored foods that are often high in refined sugars and processed grains. Here are the core principles of this diet:

Cut-OutThis includes avoiding white bread, pasta, rice, and any other foods made with white flour. The idea is that these foods can quickly raise blood sugar levels, leading to increased fat storage and other health issues.

- ***Cut-Out Refined Sugars***: Foods containing white, refined sugars (such as candies, baked goods, and sugary beverages) are excluded from the diet. These high-glycemic-index foods contribute to weight gain and can disrupt insulin sensitivity.
- ***Focus on Whole Foods***: Instead of white, processed foods, the diet emphasizes whole foods. This means consuming fruits, vegetables, whole grains (like quinoa, brown rice, and whole wheat), lean proteins, and healthy fats. These foods provide essential nutrients and support sustained energy levels and overall health.
- ***Incorporate Colorful Vegetables and Fruits***: The diet encourages the consumption of colorful vegetables and fruits, which are packed with vitamins, minerals, and antioxidants. Eating a rainbow of foods ensures a wide range of nutrients in the diet.
- ***Choose Healthier Carbohydrates***: Opt for carbohydrates that have a lower impact on blood sugar levels, such as whole grains, legumes, and starchy vegetables. These foods are digested more slowly, helping to keep you full and satisfied while maintaining stable blood sugar.

- ***Select Lean Proteins***: Including lean proteins (such as chicken, fish, tofu, and legumes) helps maintain muscle mass and promotes satiety, making it easier to manage weight.
- ***Limit Fat Intake to Healthy Fats***: While cutting down on unhealthy fats, the diet suggests incorporating sources of healthy fats, like avocados, nuts, seeds, and olive oil. These fats are essential for heart health and can help keep you feeling full.
- ***Stay Hydrated***: Drinking plenty of water is a key part of the diet, as staying hydrated supports metabolism, aids in digestion and helps control hunger.
- ***Moderation and Balance***: Above all, the "Eat Nothing White" diet promotes moderation and balance. It's about making healthier food choices consistently, rather than adhering to strict rules or completely eliminating certain food groups (except for white foods).

By following these principles, the "Eat Nothing White" diet aims to improve dietary habits, support weight management, and enhance overall health without making nutrition overly complicated.

Benefits of this Diet

The "Eat Nothing White Diet" focuses on the elimination of simple carbohydrates and promotes numerous benefits for your dietary habits and overall health. Here's a structured overview of its advantages:

1. **Nutrient-Rich Food Consumption:**
- *No Calorie Counting Required*: This diet plan simplifies healthy eating by eliminating the need to track calories, focusing instead on natural and organic foods rich in micronutrients like vitamins and minerals, which are generally lower in calories and carbs.
- *Increased Satiety with Complex Carbohydrates*: Foods high in complex carbohydrates promote longer satiety, reducing the tendency to overeat throughout the day.

2. **Health Benefits from Avoiding Refined Sugars and Flours:**
- *Elimination of 'Empty' Calories*: By cutting out sugar and refined flour, known for their minimal nutritional value, this diet helps reduce the intake of empty calories.
- *Stabilized Blood Sugar Levels*: The diet prevents blood sugar spikes by avoiding foods that trigger insulin release, aiding in the maintenance of balanced glucose levels.

3. **Reduction in Unhealthy Food Cravings:**

The diet targets and reduces cravings for commonly overconsumed foods like potato chips, bread, pizza, and ice cream, which are high in sugar and salt, thereby supporting better health.

4. **Encouragement Towards Healthy Carbohydrate Sources:**
- *Preference for Whole Foods*: It advocates for choosing whole grains, fruits, and vegetables over processed foods, highlighting the importance of consuming single-ingredient or whole foods for their intact nutrients and fiber.
- *Alternative Healthy Choices*: Instead of sugary drinks, it suggests opting for nutritious vegetable and fruit smoothies.

5. **Support for Managing Diabetes and Hypertension:**
- *Potential for Disease Management*: This diet can aid in managing diabetes and hypertension by reducing sugar and salt intake, which is crucial for regulating blood glucose and pressure levels.
- *CDC and AHA Reports*: Highlighting alarming statistics, such as over 100 million Americans living with diabetes or prediabetes and around 103 million adults experiencing high blood pressure, the diet underscores the significance of avoiding white foods and excessive sodium to combat these prevalent health issues.

Overall, the "Eat Nothing White Diet" promotes healthier eating by prioritizing nutrient-dense foods, minimizing sugar and salt intake, and encouraging choices that lead to better well-being and disease management.

Disadvantages

While the "Eat Nothing White Diet" offers benefits for healthier eating habits, it has its drawbacks. Here's a breakdown of the cons associated with this diet strategy:

1. **Misunderstanding Carbohydrates:**
- *Perceived Negatively*: Some may incorrectly assume that all carbohydrates are bad, overlooking that carbohydrates are essential energy sources. Good alternatives like brown rice and whole-wheat bread offer more nutrients and fiber compared to their white counterparts.
- Importance of Natural Foods: The emphasis remains on consuming foods in their natural state, such as whole wheat over white bread, and brown over white rice, for their health benefits.
2. **Overgeneralization of White Foods:**
- Avoidance of Healthy White Foods: There's a risk of mistakenly avoiding healthy white-colored foods such as turnips, cauliflower, and radishes due to their color, despite their nutritional value.
- Non-white Foods Can Be Unhealthy Too: It's crucial to recognize that foods of other colors, like red meats, can pose health risks if consumed excessively,

highlighting the need for a balanced nutrition evaluation.

3. **Exclusion of Beneficial Food Groups:**
- Protein Sources: Excluding certain proteins like chicken breasts, which are beneficial for weight management and muscle building due to their low-fat and high-protein content, may not be advantageous.
- Nutrient-Rich Dairy Products: Dairy products, offering calcium and other vital nutrients, are also excluded, which could lead to missed nutritional benefits.

4. **Lack of Focus on Exercise and Alternative Weight Loss Methods:**
- Underemphasized Exercise: The diet might not sufficiently stress the importance of exercise as part of a comprehensive weight management strategy. Regular physical activity is crucial for maintaining weight and overall health.
- Exploring Other Natural Weight Loss Options: Incorporating strategies like intermittent fasting or consuming green tea could complement the diet effectively without compromising its principles or health.

In summary, while the "Eat Nothing White Diet" encourages healthier eating by eliminating simple carbs and sugars, it's important to address its limitations by understanding the role of carbohydrates, considering the nutritional benefits of excluded food groups, and incorporating exercise and other natural weight loss methods into one's lifestyle for a balanced approach to health and wellness.

What Are the Things to Be Considered

After learning the basics of this diet, you need to assess if this diet plan is appropriate for you to follow. Some diets may not be designed for some people and the Eat Nothing White Diet is not an exemption.

Know its pros and cons before you decide if this diet strategy will work for you. Then devise a plan – one that is attainable, measurable, and timely. Set realistic goals that can be achieved within a prescribed period. But before making a plan, check all the things that should be done. This is to avoid conflicts before, during, and after the implementation of the diet program.

Considerations

Here are the things that need to be considered before deciding to go on a Eat Nothing White s Diet:

1. **Age and Weight**

   To safely follow this diet program, you must be between 18 to 50 years old. Younger people have a developing metabolism that could affect growth. The Eat Nothing White Diet, which reduces carbs and calories, may not be suitable for growing children or young adults. Carbs are essential for the energy needs of the younger generation, and cutting them could lead to underweight problems or stunted growth.

   For those over 50, a slower metabolism and weaker immune system could be negatively impacted by this diet. Older adults have unique health requirements that this diet might not meet. Additionally, you should weigh at least 150 pounds to start this diet plan.

2. **Overall Health**

   Even if your weight exceeds the normal range, it does not guarantee you safe access to the program. Remember that your health matters a lot and it should be a top priority. If you have existing diseases that require a balanced diet, you can't enter this diet program.

   As with any other diet plan, you should ask your physician, nutritionist, or dietician if it is safe for you to follow the Eat Nothing White s Diet.

3. **Allergies**

   People have allergies to different food types. Make sure the foods included in the diet program are ok for you to consume. Check your allergies to different food groups – especially seafood and meat. Though there are just rare cases of vegetable and fruit allergies, you still need to check if you have one. Visit your allergist/immunologist and be tested.

4. **Food Choices**

   Foods that are not your personal favorites may be required to be consumed during the program course. You need to be adaptive to these abrupt changes and decide immediately if you're up to the challenge. There is a wide range of food choices in the program. Choose the ones that you're willing to take and reserve some emergency choices.

5. **Financial Resources**

   Some food in the plan can be costly – especially those that require special herbs and spices. Be flexible; know your financial capability and choose the ones that are within your budget. Explore choices and settle for less yet equally effective food recipes.

   Remember that the amount of calories does not matter in The Eat Nothing White Diet. What truly matters are the foods you are consuming. Invest in good food choices and do not count the number of calories. You will just be required to eat a portion of each food type.

Overeating is undeniably a bad habit. It is crucial to cultivate strong self-discipline to adhere to your diet plan. The most challenging aspect of any diet is maintaining consistency until you reach your goals.

At the beginning of the "Eat Nothing White" diet, it's particularly easy to stray from your path, which means you'll need a robust strategy to stay motivated. It's important to remember that this diet not only helps in shedding and managing weight but also enhances your overall health and ward off diseases.

5 Step-by-Step Guide on How to Start the 'Eat Nothing White' Diet

The 'Eat Nothing White' diet is a straightforward and impactful approach to revamping your eating habits, focusing on eliminating white foods—typically high in refined sugars and flours—from your diet. This change can lead to improved blood sugar levels, better digestion, and even weight loss. Here's how you can get started:

Step 1: Understand What 'White' Foods Are

Kicking off your journey with the 'Eat Nothing White' diet begins with a crucial understanding of what constitutes 'white' foods. These items are primarily those made from white flour or sugar, which include a wide array of commonly consumed products such as bread, pasta, rice, pastries, sweets, and certain dairy products like some cheeses and milk that haveEat added sugar.

It's important to acknowledge that 'white' foods also extend to processed foods such as crackers, snack bars, and most fast-food options. The refinement process these foods undergo strips them of nutritional value, leaving behind simple carbohydrates that can spike your blood sugar levels and lead to energy crashes.

Identifying these 'white' foods within your current diet is essential. Take a detailed inventory of your pantry and refrigerator, noting items that fall under this category. This exercise isn't just about recognizing what to eliminate but also understanding how prevalent refined and processed foods are in your diet.

The ultimate goal here is not only to avoid these 'white' foods but to pivot towards a diet rich in whole, unprocessed foods. These healthier alternatives not only provide your body with essential nutrients and fiber but also support stable blood sugar levels and a sustainable energy supply. By committing to this initial step, you're laying a solid foundation for a healthier lifestyle that transcends dieting, moving towards comprehensive well-being.

Step 2: Clear Out Your Pantry

After pinpointing the 'white' foods lurking in your kitchen, the next pivotal action is purging your pantry of these items. This cleansing process is more than a mere cleanup; it's a symbolic gesture of your dedication to a healthier lifestyle.

While the idea of discarding food may initially feel wasteful or overwhelming, reframe this step as an opportunity for renewal and transformation. By removing these unhealthy options, you create physical and mental space for nourishing alternatives that align with your dietary goals. Consider donating any unopened, non-perishable 'white' foods to local food banks.

This not only assists you in decluttering but also serves a dual purpose of aiding those in need. Such an act of kindness reinforces the positive impact of your dietary shift, extending its benefits beyond your own health and into the community.

Step 3: Stock Up on Whole Food Alternatives

Now that your pantry space has been revitalized by clearing out the 'white' foods, it's the perfect moment to replenish with whole food alternatives. Embark on this exciting phase by selecting whole grains over their refined counterparts.

Replace white bread and rice with nutrient-rich versions like whole grain bread, brown rice, or even quinoa, which offer a complex carbohydrate source for sustained energy. Explore the diverse world of pasta made from legumes (such as chickpeas or lentils) and whole grains, which not only adhere to the 'eat nothing white' rule but also amp up your protein intake.

Venture further into this dietary transformation by incorporating a colorful array of vegetables and fruits into your meals. These natural powerhouses are brimming with vitamins, minerals, and fiber, essential for optimal health. Lean into sources of lean proteins—think poultry, fish, beans, and legumes—to build and repair tissues, while healthy fats from avocados, nuts, and seeds round out your diet, supporting brain health and satiety.

By consciously choosing these whole food alternatives, you're not just adhering to a rule; you're investing in your body's long-term wellness. These swaps introduce a spectrum of flavors and textures to your plate, making your dietary transition both healthful and delightful.

Step 4: Plan Your Meals

Diving into meal planning is a pivotal strategy in successfully adhering to the 'eat nothing white' diet. Initiating this step involves setting aside time each week to thoughtfully map out your meals, ensuring a diverse intake of whole foods. This approach allows you to maintain a balanced diet rich in nutrients, flavors, and textures, making every meal an opportunity to nourish your body and delight your senses.

Begin by exploring the vast array of recipes and resources available online, specifically those catering to whole-food diets. These can serve as a wellspring of inspiration, offering creative ideas on how to combine whole grains, vegetables, fruits, lean proteins, and healthy fats into delicious meals. Variety is key to keeping your diet engaging and satisfying, helping to fend off monotony and the subsequent temptation to revert to convenient but unhealthy 'white' foods.

Craft your weekly menu with mindfulness, considering the balance of macronutrients and the inclusion of all food groups. Planning ahead also streamlines grocery shopping, ensuring you have all the necessary ingredients on hand, which further reinforces your commitment to healthier eating habits. Meal planning is not just a dietary tool; it's a lifestyle adjustment that fosters discipline, creativity, and a deeper connection to the foods you consume.

Step 5: Monitor Your Progress and Adjust Accordingly

The final, crucial step in your 'eat nothing white' diet is to diligently monitor your progress. This involves more than just observing changes in your weight or body shape; it's about tuning into your body's responses to this dietary shift.

Keep a journal or use a digital app to record not just what you eat, but also how you feel physically and emotionally. This reflective practice can highlight correlations between your diet and changes in energy levels, mood swings, sleep quality, and overall sense of well-being.

Patience is paramount during this phase. Transformative changes often unfold gradually, so give yourself grace and time to adapt. It's normal to encounter hurdles or moments of temptation. Instead of viewing these as failures, see them as opportunities to learn and refine your approach.

If certain restrictions prove too challenging or if you find gaps in your nutritional intake, be flexible in adjusting your strategy. Perhaps introducing a wider variety of whole grains, experimenting with new vegetables, or adjusting portion sizes could reinvigorate your commitment and results.

Remember, the essence of the 'eat nothing white' diet lies in fostering healthier food choices, not in adhering to stringent rules. As you evolve with your diet, your dietary habits should evolve too, always aiming to enhance your health and happiness.

By following these five steps, you can successfully start and maintain the 'eat nothing white' diet. Remember, this dietary change is a step towards a healthier lifestyle. Listen to your body, be flexible with your approach, and enjoy discovering the variety and flavors that whole foods offer.

Foods to Eat

The following are the food groups that can be included in the no-white foods diet.

1. **Fruits and Vegetables**

    All fruits and vegetables are safe to eat except for some types of beans and potatoes. Potatoes and beans contain high carbohydrates and glucose that can be easily deposited into the blood vessels. Naturally, white vegetables such as cauliflower and parsnips are exceptions to this no-white policy. Fruits and vegetables should be eaten raw or half-cooked.

2. **Grains and Cereals**

   Whole grains and cereals contain less sugar which can be a good substitute for rice and regular pasta. Brown rice and oatmeal are more nutritious grain choices for no-white food dieters. Whole wheat pasta and grain bread are also a good source of healthier carbs that can be included in the diet.

   Foods made from whole grain have higher fiber content which is essential to regular bowel movement. These also contain complex carbohydrates which take a longer time to absorb so you feel full longer.

3. **Protein and Dairy Products**

   Animal meat, including white meat which is a good source of protein, is included in the No White Diet. Meat like beef, chicken, and pork are good sources of protein and other nutrients. Fish is also included in the allowed foods.

   Eggs can also be eaten – even the white portion of the egg. As for dairy products, some experts suggest including milk in the diet while others do not recommend it. Take note that cheese and butter are not at all allowed in this type of diet.

Foods to Avoid

The "Eat Nothing White" diet emphasizes consuming foods in their most natural state, steering clear of certain foods to make healthier choices. Here's a more organized look at what to avoid on this diet:

1. **Primary White Foods to Exclude**
- Refined Grains and Sugars

   This category includes white rice, white bread, white potatoes, flour, and other similar white food products. These items are high in simple carbohydrates and sugars, contributing to quick digestion but short-lived satiety, leading to increased calorie consumption and potential weight gain.

- High-Carb and High-Sugar Foods

   The diet avoids foods that are low in nutrients but high in calories and sugar, which are not beneficial for health.

2. **Naturally White Foods**

   Dairy Products: Items like butter and cheese, though naturally white, are recommended to be eliminated or minimized due to their fat content and potential to disrupt the diet's goals.

3. Artificial Sweeteners and Processed Juices

Artificial sweeteners and powdered fruit juices are also on the avoidance list, as they can trigger cravings for sugary foods. Despite their low or non-existent calorie count, these substitutes may increase the desire for high-sugar snacks.

4. Satisfying Sweet Cravings Healthily

For sweet cravings, opt for whole fruits or unsweetened pineapple juice, which can offer sweetness along with beneficial fiber.

Hidden Sugars to Watch For: Be vigilant about various names for sugar found in syrups, concentrates, and other foods. Common ones include:

- Brown, cane, invert, and coconut sugar
- Evaporated cane juice, beet sugar, agave, and maple syrup
- Juice concentrates from grapes or apples
- Rice syrup, Demerara, honey, piloncillo/panela
- Sucanat, muscovado, turbinado Additionally, ingredients ending in "-ose" (such as glucose, sucrose, fructose, dextrose, lactose) indicate the presence of sugar.

Sugar might be hiding in the foods you usually buy from the supermarket so you must read the label thoroughly if you want to follow the Eat Nothing White Diet plan.

The Eat Nothing White Diet Food Guide

The Eat Nothing White Diet program should start with a meal plan—one that lists all the possible food choices to be included in the diet program. As a no-white-food dieter, your main responsibility is to stick to your chosen program until the end. Here is the list of different food choices that can be included in the diet program. You can use this as your guide.

Breakfast

Some people consider themselves as non-breakfast persons while some can't live without 'the most important meal of the day'. If you're used to eating "like a king" for breakfast, that has to change when you begin with your new diet program.

Most breakfast items are white foods like white bread and pastries that are also laden with white sugar. Follow this guide to choose the most appropriate breakfast food in the no white-foods program. **Remember: DO NOT SKIP BREAKFAST!**

Foods to Eat

- Whole Wheat Bread or Cereal
- Eggs
- Half-sliced fruit (any kind)
- Coffee (but should only be 1 cup of about 200ml)
- Water

Foods to Avoid

- Pancakes, bread, biscuits, syrups
- Energy and vitamin bars
- Processed meats
- Fruit juices
- Jelly, honey, jam

Mid-Morning Snack

Eating snacks should not be taken for granted when following an Eat Nothing White diet. This will give you extra energy when you need it. Eating sensible and healthy snacks helps reduce the amount of food you consume on the next full meal.

Unfortunately, most snacks that you have been used to are considered white foods like crackers and chips. They might be tasty but they're full of processed carbs and they lack nutrients. Instead, go for the following food items:

Foods to Eat

- Almonds, pistachio nuts, assorted tree nuts

- Banana or apple
- Water

Foods to Avoid

- Sodas
- Candies and chocolates
- Processed chips
- Junk foods

Lunch

If you're a light breakfast eater and have no time for a snack in between, you tend to go heavy for your lunch. Lunch is the perfect time to incorporate meat into your diet. You can also eat heavily during lunchtime but not to the extent of overeating.

Foods to Eat

- All kinds of meat – broiled or grilled
- Brown rice about ¼ cup (50g)
- Fish, tuna
- Vegetable and fruit salad
- 1 slice of raw vegetables (any kind)
- ½ slice fruit (any kind)
- Water, tea

Foods to Avoid

- Hamburger, fries

- Bread
- Sauces
- Fruit juices, sodas

Mid-Afternoon Snack

- Same as the mid-morning snack

Supper

Eating heavily for dinner is likely to result in weight gain and obesity. Metabolism slows down in the evening and more so when you are sleeping because it's usually the time when you are at home and relaxing, thus consuming less energy.

Supper is a time when you will need to eat smaller portions for better digestion. If you eat more than recommended, the extra calories will be stored in your body as fat and will find their way around your waist. Eat light so your body doesn't need to overwork to digest the food as you sleep.

Foods to Eat

- Any kind of meat – broiled or grilled
- Fish and tuna
- Seafood
- ½ slice veggie
- ¼ slice fruit
- Water, unsweetened tea

Foods to Avoid
- Anything fried
- Corn
- Potatoes
- Beer and hard liquor

Bedtime snacks are not at all recommended. After supper, you should take a couple of walking steps. After walking, drink 1 glass of warm water to facilitate a good flow of nutrients within your body systems. Never drink wine and other types of alcoholic drinks before sleeping. Alcohol may initially make you drowsy, but it can wake you up in the middle of the night feeling restless.

Making Smarter Choices – Week 1

The Eat Nothing White Diet program is easier compared to other diet programs. This is because you still get to enjoy different food sources and not deprive yourself of your usual favorites. With this diet, you just need to be smarter about the food choices that you make.

Skipping any mealtime of the day is not evident in this kind of diet program. That means you don't have to starve because you're waiting for a particular time window to eat as you would in an intermittent fasting diet program.

This guide has provided weekly lists of activities to follow in the whole course of the Eat Nothing White Diet program. You just need to follow these wholeheartedly – including the recipes, menus, and other activities.

The First Week

The 1st week is the most crucial in the Eat Nothing White Diet program. Your body will start to adjust to the new sets of food being introduced into your system. This stage is particularly challenging for people who have been used to consuming white foods as a staple source of their caloric needs. This is your body's natural reaction to the changes in your regular food consumption.

You may experience food cravings, especially for sugar and starch, but you need to learn how to resist temptations. But as you consume less of these foods in your Eat Nothing White Diet journey, you'll feel the cravings becoming less frequent until they're completely gone. Stick to your goal and just continue.

Motivate yourself by keeping in mind that you're doing this to get and keep healthy. Remember to check all the considerations before entering the diet program. Refer to Chapter 2 for your guide.

What to Eat

Breakfast

Since this is your first week in the program, you need not be deprived of the food you typically eat. If it is not included in this list, you may freely eat it on the very first day of the first week. The first day of the first week is your "liberty" moment. You can eat the following for breakfast freely:

(Remember, only on the first day!)

- 1 slice of whole-wheat bread
- 1-2 pcs. boiled or poached egg

- 1 small bowl of cereal
- 1 cup of coffee (200 ml) or ½ cup of milk (100-150ml)
- 1 slice of your favorite fruit and vegetable
- 1 glass of water (250-300ml)

On the 2nd–7th day of the first week, you can eat the following breakfast combos alternately. Please strictly follow.

- Combo 1: ½ slice plain whole wheat bread (not heated); 1 pc boiled egg; ½ slice green apple; 1 glass of lukewarm water
- Combo 2: ½ small bowl of no-sugar, low-carb cereal (about 120mg) mixed with ½ cup of milk (about 125ml); ½ slice of apple; 1 glass of lukewarm water
- Do not drink coffee!

Note: Strictly follow the next meal recipes and menus

Mid-Morning Snack

It is highly recommended to eat different varieties of healthy nuts during snack times. In the first week, you can consume the following in your mid-morning snacks:

- Days 1, 3, 5, 7: 10-15 pcs fresh hazelnuts
- Days 2, 4, 6: 10-15 pcs fresh walnuts
- 1 glass of fresh water

Lunch

It is advisable to just eat 1 set of lunch menus during the first week. Doing so can make your body more adaptive to the new set of nutrients being introduced.

This is also to ensure that your body receives the minimum and safe amount of sugar and calories daily. In the 1st week of the program, eat the following foods during lunchtime:

- No White Vegetable Salad & Grilled Tuna
- 1 glass of fresh water (not cold)

No White Veggies Salad

Ingredients:

- 1/2 pc cucumber, peeled and chopped thinly
- 2 pcs red tomatoes, chopped
- 5 pcs Romaine lettuce leaves, torn into pieces
- 2 pcs regular-sized onions, minced
- 1 small-sized red bell pepper, chopped
- 1 pc carrots, chopped
- 1/2 small-sized clove garlic, minced
- 1 tbsp. lemon juice
- a pinch of salt
- 1 tsp. water

Instructions:

1. In a mixing bowl, mix all the ingredients using a spatula or a mixing spoon.
2. Do not add any salad dressings such as mayonnaise or balsamic vinegar. The lemon juice and salt are enough to add flavor to your salad.
3. Consume immediately.

For Grilled Tuna, follow these 3 easy steps:

1. Marinate 1 slice of tuna using 3 tsp lemon juice, 1 pc minced garlic, salt, and pepper.
2. Grill for 5-7 minutes
3. Serve.

Mid-Afternoon Snack

- Days 1, 3, 5, 7: 10-15 pcs fresh almonds
- Days 2, 4, 6: 10-15 pcs fresh Brazil nuts
- 1 glass of fresh water

Supper

The goal is to eat less during supper to avoid extra deposits of carbohydrates in the blood vessels. This is also to facilitate good digestion and easy bowel movement the following day. Here are the recommended menu options for supper on the first week of Eat Nothing White's Diet:

- Easy Garlic Broiled Chicken
- 10 pcs black grapes
- 1 glass of water

Easy Garlic Broiled Chicken

Ingredients:

- 2 pcs skinless chicken breasts
- 1 tbsp. lemon juice
- 1/2 tsp. pepper powder
- 3 cloves garlic, minced
- a pinch of salt

Instructions:

1. Preheat broiler.
2. In a small bowl, mix together lemon juice, pepper powder, garlic, and salt.
3. Place chicken breasts on a baking dish and pour the mixture over them, making sure to coat both sides evenly.
4. Broil for 5-7 minutes on each side or until cooked through. Serve with black grapes and a glass of water for a balanced supper meal.

Note: You can also use this recipe for grilled tuna and simply replace the lemon juice with the marinade mixture. Serve with a side of fresh greens for a complete and nutritious meal.

Besides following the recommended meals, it is also important to stay hydrated throughout the day by drinking plenty of water. Additionally, incorporating regular exercise into your daily routine can further enhance the benefits of the Eat Nothing White Diet.

The Reinforcement Period – Week 2

Week 1 serves as the adjustment phase of the diet program, where individuals begin to adapt to their new eating habits. In Week 2, known as the reinforcement phase, participants are encouraged to diversify their diet by incorporating a variety of healthier carbohydrates and proteins. This diversification ensures the body receives the essential nutrients it requires.

During this period, it's common to observe initial weight loss, typically in the range of 10-15 lbs., which is a positive sign of progress. However, a weight loss exceeding 25 lbs. should be viewed with caution, as it could indicate an excessively rapid reduction. To counteract this, the focus of Week 2 revolves around reinforcing the intake of nutritious carbs and quality proteins, alongside engaging in effective exercises designed to enhance calorie burning and accelerate the weight loss process.

Important Note: If you do not experience weight loss in the first week, it's recommended to restart the program from Day 1.

What to Eat

Breakfast

For Week 2, breakfast menu plans are similar to those on Week 1. The number of servings will just be increased by half or may be doubled. You will alternately use these breakfast combos from days 1-7.

- Days 1, 3, 5, 7: 1 slice plain whole wheat bread (not heated); 1 ½ boiled egg; 1 slice of green apple; 1 glass of lukewarm water
- Days 2, 4, 6: 1 bowl of no sugar, low-carb cereal (about 240 mg) mixed with (still) ½ cup of milk (about 125ml); 1 slice of apple; 1 glass of lukewarm water
- Do not drink coffee!

Mid-Morning Snack

- Days 1 – 7: 10-15 pcs Brazil nuts and 10-15 pcs Macadamia nuts
- 1 glass of fresh water

Lunch

Days 1 and 7

- 1 small bowl of Garlic Spinach – about 250 grams
- Grilled Lamb – 5 thin strips
- 1 glass of water

Days 2, 3, 4, 5, 6

- Use the lunch menus in Week 1
- Garlic Spinach
- Grilled Lamb

Since this is a diet program, consume only the recommended amount/servings. Remember, do not overeat!

Mid-Afternoon Snack

- Days 1 – 7: 10-15 pcs pecans and 10-15 pcs almonds
- 1 glass of fresh water

Supper

Days 1, 3, 5, 7

- 1/2 cup of brown rice
- Easy Garlic Broiled Chicken/Pork
- 10 pcs black grapes, 5 pcs. strawberry
- 1 glass of water

Days 2, 4, 6

- 1/2 cup of brown rice
- Grilled Salmon
- 10 pcs strawberry, 1 whole orange
- 1 glass of water

Recipes can be found in the Week 1 program. For broiled pork, follow the same steps in making broiled chicken.

After supper, do not eat anything—especially chips, chocolates, candies, and junk foods. Before sleeping, drink 1 cup of warm, unsweetened jasmine tea.

Physical Activity

Relying solely on dieting is insufficient for achieving optimal results in a weight loss journey. Incorporating exercises, including walking, running, and weightlifting, is crucial. Consider joining a gym and engaging a fitness instructor to guide you effectively.

The Maintenance Period – Week 3

Week 3 serves as the crucial maintenance phase. Diligently adhering to the guidelines established in Weeks 1 and 2 sets the stage for success within this dietary plan. Cultivating the habit of logging your daily weight is instrumental in monitoring your progression throughout the program.

At this juncture, the Eat Nothing White Diet begins to manifest noticeable improvements in your physical well-being. By Week 3, your body should have seamlessly adapted to the dietary modifications introduced. Should you encounter any setbacks, however, reverting to Day 1 of Week 1 remains a viable option.

Food Choices

You can freely choose the type of food you're going to consume at this point. Just follow the right food measurements and servings to get the same amount of nutrients needed by your body. To help you choose, these might be helpful:

- Ensure your diet is balanced with healthy carbohydrates, proteins, and essential micronutrients.
- Incorporate a variety of fruits and vegetables into every meal.
- Hydration is key; opt for water primarily. If you choose to add fruit juices, which are permissible in Week 3, keep it to no more than ½ glass (120ml).
- For snacks, opt for healthy tree nuts like macadamia and almonds, steering clear of peanuts.
- Exclude coffee, wine, and beer from your diet, and limit milk consumption to one glass.

Alternative Recipes

Aside from the ones featured in the previous chapters, you can also make use of the following recipes.

Green Salad

Ingredients:

- 1 cup of green lettuce
- 1/2 cup of chopped tomatoes
- 1/2 cucumber peeled and sliced into thin pieces.
- A few slices of carrot for added nutrients

Instructions:

1. Wash the lettuce leaves and place them in a bowl.
2. Add chopped tomatoes, cucumber, and carrot slices.
3. Toss lightly.
4. You can add salt, pepper, and a dash of olive oil for dressing.

Rosemary Veggies - Roasted

Ingredients:

- 3 cups of a mixture of chopped vegetables (carrots, bell peppers, zucchini)
- 2 Tbsp. of olive oil
- 1 teaspoon of dried rosemary
- Salt and pepper to taste

Instructions:

1. Preheat the oven to 400°F (200°C).
2. Toss the chopped vegetables in a bowl with olive oil, dried rosemary, salt, and pepper.
3. Spread the vegetables evenly on a baking sheet and roast for 20 minutes or until tender.
4. Serve hot as a side dish or add to salads.

Exercise

Simple activities like walking, jogging, cycling, or swimming can complement your diet program effectively. Beyond calorie burning, these exercises enhance mood and mental sharpness, boost the immune system, and strengthen bones and muscles.

Remember, Week 3 is not the conclusion of the Eat Nothing White Diet program. In the coming weeks, the key is creativity in both meal planning and exercising to sustain your ideal weight.

Explore the Bonus Recipes section for additional culinary inspiration. To prevent monotony, it's important to vary your weekly meals. Use these recipes to craft your dishes, keeping in mind the diet's dos and don'ts.

Achieving a healthy body weight and BMI signifies overall fitness and well-being. Cutting out white foods can significantly reduce calorie intake, thereby lowering the risk of diabetes and heart disease. Allow the Eat Nothing White Diet plan to steer you towards your health objectives.

Bonus Recipes

We have included some bonus recipes for you to try out during your Eat Nothing White Diet journey. These recipes are delicious, nutritious, and most importantly, white food-free!

Salmon and Salad Mix

Ingredients:

- 4 salmon filets (about 6 ounces each)
- 2 Tbsp. olive oil
- 1 teaspoon paprika
- Salt and pepper to taste
- 1 large avocado, sliced
- 2 cups mixed greens (such as spinach, arugula, and kale)
- 1/2 cup cherry tomatoes, halved
- 1/4 cup red onion, thinly sliced
- 1/4 cup cucumber, sliced
- 1/4 cup carrots, shredded
- 1/2 lemon, for dressing
- 2 Tbsp. balsamic vinegar
- 1 Tbsp. Dijon mustard (make sure it's without added sugars)
- 1 garlic clove, minced

Instructions:

1. Preheat the Grill or Oven: When utilizing a grill, warm it up to a medium-high setting before use. For oven preparation, preheat your oven to 375°F (190°C).
2. Prepare the Salmon: Rinse the salmon filets under cold water and pat them dry with paper towels. Rub each

filet with 1 Tbsp. of olive oil. Season with paprika, salt, and pepper.

Cook the Salmon:

3. For Grilling: Place the salmon on the grill, skin-side down. Grill for about 6-8 minutes per side, or until the salmon flakes easily with a fork.
4. For Baking: Place the salmon in a baking dish and bake for about 12-15 minutes, or until cooked through and flaky.
5. Prepare the Salad: In a large bowl, combine the mixed greens, cherry tomatoes, red onion, cucumber, and carrots. Toss the ingredients to mix well.
6. Make the Dressing: Mix the final tablespoon of olive oil, balsamic vinegar, Dijon mustard, minced garlic, and a bit of lemon juice in a small bowl, whisking thoroughly. Season to taste with salt and pepper.
7. Assemble the Dish: Place a generous portion of the salad mix on each plate. Top with sliced avocado and a grilled or baked salmon filet. Drizzle the dressing over the salad and salmon before serving.
8. Serve: Enjoy your hearty and healthy Salmon and Salad Mix, perfect for the No White Foods Diet!

Homemade Mexican Bowl

Ingredients:

- 1 pound lean ground turkey
- 1 Tbsp. olive oil
- 1 teaspoon cumin
- 1 teaspoon chili powder
- 1/2 teaspoon garlic powder
- Salt and pepper to taste
- 1 cup brown rice, cooked
- 1 can black beans (15 oz), rinsed and drained
- 1 cup corn kernels (fresh, frozen and thawed, or canned without sugar)
- 1 avocado, diced
- 1 cup cherry tomatoes, halved
- 1/4 cup red onion, finely chopped
- 1/4 cup fresh cilantro, chopped
- Juice of 1 lime
- 1/2 cup salsa (ensure it's without added sugars)
- 1/2 cup plain Greek yogurt (as a sour cream substitute)

Instructions:

1. Cook the Turkey: Heat the olive oil in a large skillet over medium heat. Add the ground turkey, breaking it apart with a spoon. Cook until browned, about 5-7 minutes. Drain any excess fat.

2. Season the Turkey: Add cumin, chili powder, garlic powder, salt, and pepper to the skillet with the turkey. Stir well to combine and cook for another 2 minutes. Remove from heat and set aside.
3. Prepare the Brown Rice: Cook the brown rice according to package instructions if not pre-cooked. Ensure you're using brown rice as it's whole grain and permitted in the "Eat Nothing White" diet.
4. Assemble the Bowls: Divide the cooked brown rice among four bowls. Top each bowl with an equal amount of seasoned ground turkey, black beans, corn kernels, avocado, cherry tomatoes, and red onion.
5. Add Toppings: Sprinkle fresh cilantro over each bowl. Squeeze fresh lime juice over each and top with a dollop of salsa and Greek yogurt.
6. Serve: Enjoy your Homemade Mexican Bowl, a colorful and nutritious meal that fits perfectly within the "Eat Nothing White" diet guidelines!

Broccoli and Beans Soup

Ingredients:

- 2 Tbsp.s olive oil
- 1 medium onion, chopped (choose red or yellow onion instead of white to adhere to the diet restrictions)
- 2 cloves garlic, minced
- 4 cups broccoli florets (fresh or frozen)
- 1 can (15 oz) cannellini beans or chickpeas, rinsed and drained (ensure no added sugar or preservatives)
- 4 cups vegetable broth (check for no added sugars or white starches)
- 1 teaspoon dried thyme
- Salt and pepper to taste
- 1 bay leaf
- Juice of half a lemon
- Optional garnish: chopped parsley or chives

Instructions:

1. Sauté the Onion and Garlic: In a large pot, heat the olive oil over medium heat. Add the chopped onion and sauté until translucent, about 4-5 minutes. Add the minced garlic and cook for another minute until fragrant.
2. Cook the Broccoli: Add the broccoli florets to the pot along with the dried thyme, salt, and pepper. Sauté for

3-4 minutes, just until the broccoli starts to turn bright green.
3. Add Beans and Broth: Stir in the cannellini beans or chickpeas and the vegetable broth. Add the bay leaf. Bring the mixture to a boil, then reduce the heat to low and simmer for about 15-20 minutes, or until the broccoli is tender.
4. Blend the Soup: Once the broccoli is tender, remove the bay leaf. Use an immersion blender to blend the soup directly in the pot, or carefully transfer the soup to a blender and blend until smooth. If using a blender, return the soup to the pot after blending.
5. Season and Serve: Add the lemon juice to the soup and adjust the seasoning with more salt and pepper if needed. Serve hot, garnished with chopped parsley or chives if desired.

Beef Sirloin Tips in Pepper Sauce

Ingredients:

- 2 pounds beef sirloin tips, slice into small, manageable pieces
- 2 Tbsp. olive oil, divided
- Salt and black pepper to taste
- 1 red bell pepper, thinly sliced
- 1 yellow bell pepper, thinly sliced
- 1 green bell pepper, thinly sliced
- 1 medium onion, sliced (choose red or yellow onion instead of white to adhere to the diet restrictions)
- 2 cloves garlic, minced
- 1 cup beef broth (ensure no added sugars or artificial ingredients)
- 2 tablespoons balsamic vinegar
- 1 tablespoon low-sodium soy sauce (or coconut aminos for a gluten-free option)
- 1 teaspoon Dijon mustard (check for no added sugars)
- 1/2 teaspoon smoked paprika
- Optional garnish: chopped parsley or chives

Instructions:

1. Prepare the Beef: Season the beef sirloin tips with salt and black pepper.
2. Brown the Beef: In a large skillet, heat 1 tablespoon of olive oil over medium-high heat. Add the beef in

batches, searing each piece on all sides until browned but not cooked through. Remove the beef from the skillet and set aside.

3. Sauté the Vegetables: In the same skillet, add the remaining tablespoon of olive oil. Add the sliced bell peppers and onion, sautéing over medium heat until they start to soften, about 5 minutes. Add the garlic and cook for an additional minute until fragrant.
4. Create the Pepper Sauce: Add the beef broth, balsamic vinegar, low-sodium soy sauce (or coconut aminos), Dijon mustard, and smoked paprika to the skillet with the vegetables. Stir well to combine all the ingredients. Bring the mixture to a simmer.
5. Combine and Cook: Return the beef sirloin tips to the skillet, stirring to coat them in the sauce and vegetables. Reduce the heat to low and simmer for about 10 minutes, or until the beef is cooked to your desired level of doneness and the sauce has slightly thickened.
6. Serve: Remove the skillet from the heat. Taste and adjust the seasoning if necessary. Serve the beef sirloin tips in pepper sauce hot, garnished with chopped parsley or chives if using.

Lemon-Ginger Chicken

Ingredients:

- 4 boneless, skinless chicken breasts
- 2 Tbsp. olive oil
- Salt and black pepper to taste
- 2 lemons, juiced and zested
- 2 Tbsp. fresh ginger, grated
- 3 cloves garlic, minced
- 1 Tbsp. soy sauce (or coconut aminos for a gluten-free option)
- 1 teaspoon honey (ensure it's pure, with no added sugars)
- 1/2 cup chicken broth (check for no added sugars or artificial ingredients)
- Optional garnish: fresh parsley or cilantro, chopped

Instructions:

1. Prepare the Chicken: Season both sides of the chicken breasts with salt and black pepper.
2. Cook the Chicken: In a large skillet, heat the olive oil over medium-high heat. Add the chicken breasts and cook for about 5-7 minutes on each side or until golden brown and cooked through. Remove the chicken from the skillet and set aside, keeping it warm.
3. Make the Lemon-Ginger Sauce: In the same skillet, reduce the heat to medium. Add the lemon juice,

lemon zest, grated ginger, minced garlic, soy sauce (or coconut aminos), and honey. Stir to combine all the ingredients, scraping up any browned bits from the bottom of the skillet.
4. Add Chicken Broth: Pour in the chicken broth and stir well. Bring the mixture to a simmer and allow it to cook for about 2-3 minutes, or until slightly thickened.
5. Return Chicken to Skillet: Add the cooked chicken breasts back to the skillet, spooning the lemon-ginger sauce over them. Cook for another 2-3 minutes, ensuring the chicken is well coated and heated through.
6. Serve: Transfer the chicken to serving plates. Spoon extra sauce over the top and garnish with chopped parsley or cilantro if desired.

Grilled Teriyaki Chicken

Ingredients:

- 4 boneless, skinless chicken breasts
- 1/4 cup low-sodium soy sauce (ensure it's naturally brewed with no added sugars)
- 2 tablespoons of apple cider vinegar
- 2 tablespoons of water
- 1 tablespoon of freshly grated ginger
- 2 cloves garlic, minced
- 1 tablespoon of honey (or to taste, as a natural sweetener alternative)
- 1 teaspoon of sesame oil
- 1 tablespoon of finely chopped green onions (for garnish)
- Sesame seeds (for garnish; optional)

Instructions:

1. For the marinade: In a mixing bowl, combine the low-sodium soy sauce, apple cider vinegar, water, grated ginger, minced garlic, honey, and sesame oil, whisking until everything is fully integrated.
2. Marinate the Chicken: Place the chicken breasts in a large sealable bag or container. Pour the marinade over the chicken, ensuring all pieces are well coated. Seal the bag or container and refrigerate for at least 30 minutes to 2 hours, allowing the flavors to infuse.

3. Preheat the Grill: Set your grill to a medium-high temperature before cooking. Ensure the grates are clean and lightly oiled to prevent sticking.
4. Grill the Chicken: Remove the chicken from the marinade, letting any excess drip off. Discard the remaining marinade. Grill the chicken for 6-7 minutes on each side, or until fully cooked through and the internal temperature reaches 165°F (74°C).
5. Rest and Serve: Once cooked, transfer the chicken to a plate, cover loosely with foil, and let it rest for about 5 minutes. This helps retain the juices, making the chicken more tender and flavorful.
6. Garnish and Enjoy: Slice the grilled teriyaki chicken and garnish with green onions and sesame seeds before serving.

Peach Glazed Pork Chops

Ingredients:

- 4 bone-in pork chops, about 1-inch thick
- Salt and freshly ground black pepper, to taste
- 2 tablespoons olive oil
- 3 ripe peaches, pitted and sliced (or equivalent in frozen peaches, thawed)
- 1 small red onion, finely chopped
- 2 cloves garlic, minced
- 1/4 cup balsamic vinegar
- 1 tablespoon raw honey (optional, depending on your diet's guidelines)
- 1 teaspoon fresh thyme leaves, plus more for garnish
- 1/4 cup water or low-sodium chicken broth

Instructions:

1. Prepare the Pork Chops: Season both sides of the pork chops generously with salt and freshly ground black pepper.
2. Cook Pork Chops: Heat olive oil in a large skillet over medium-high heat. Add the pork chops and cook until golden brown and cooked through, about 5-7 minutes per side, depending on thickness. Transfer to a plate and cover to keep warm.
3. Make the Peach Glaze: In the same skillet, add the sliced peaches, red onion, and garlic. Sauté for about

2-3 minutes, or until the onions are translucent and peaches start to soften.
4. Add Vinegar and Honey: Pour in the balsamic vinegar and add the raw honey (if using). Stir well to combine and dissolve the honey. Allow the mixture to simmer for about 5 minutes, or until slightly reduced and thickened.
5. Add Thyme and Water/Broth: Stir in the fresh thyme leaves and water (or chicken broth). Bring the mixture back to a simmer and cook for an additional 3-5 minutes, allowing the flavors to meld together and the sauce to thicken slightly.
6. Finish the Dish: Return the pork chops to the skillet, spooning some of the peach glaze over them. Cook for another 2-3 minutes, or until the pork chops are heated through and glazed.
7. Serve: Plate the pork chops and spoon over any remaining peach glaze from the skillet. Garnish with additional fresh thyme leaves.

Ginger Chicken Kabobs

Ingredients:

- 2 pounds chicken breast, cut into 1-inch cubes
- 1/4 cup low-sodium soy sauce (ensure it's naturally brewed with no added sugars)
- 1/4 cup olive oil
- 3 tablespoons fresh lemon juice
- 2 tablespoons fresh ginger, grated
- 3 cloves garlic, minced
- 1 tablespoon raw honey (optional, or adjusted based on dietary allowances)
- 1 red bell pepper, cut into 1-inch pieces
- 1 green bell pepper, cut into 1-inch pieces
- 1 large red onion, cut into 1-inch pieces
- Salt and freshly ground black pepper, to taste
- Fresh cilantro, chopped (for garnish)

Instructions:

1. To create the marinade: Mix low-sodium soy sauce, olive oil, lemon juice, grated ginger, minced garlic, and raw honey (optional) in a sizable bowl until thoroughly blended.
2. Marinate the Chicken: Add the cubed chicken to the marinade and toss to ensure each piece is well coated. Cover and refrigerate for at least 1 hour, or up to 4 hours for more flavor.

3. Preheat the Grill: Heat your grill to a medium-high level and gently coat the grates with oil to ensure the food doesn't stick.
4. Prepare the Kabobs: String the marinated cubes of chicken onto skewers, interspersing them with slices of red and green bell peppers and chunks of red onion. Season with salt and freshly ground black pepper to taste.
5. Grill the Kabobs: Place the kabobs on the preheated grill and cook for about 10-15 minutes, turning occasionally, until the chicken is fully cooked through and the vegetables are tender and slightly charred.
6. Serve: Remove the kabobs from the grill and allow them to rest for a few minutes. Garnish with chopped fresh cilantro before serving.

Conclusion

Congratulations on reaching the end of our "Eat Nothing White" diet guide! By now, you've taken a significant step toward understanding how limiting white foods—those often high in refined sugars and flours—can make a profound difference in your health, energy levels, and overall well-being. It's no small feat to educate yourself about making healthier food choices, and for that, you deserve a big round of applause.

The core takeaway from this guide is simple yet powerful: by cutting out or significantly reducing white foods like white bread, pasta, rice, and sugar, you can help stabilize your blood sugar levels, reduce inflammation, and potentially lose weight.

This shift towards more colorful plates isn't just about what you're taking away; it's about what you're adding. Think vibrant vegetables, lean proteins, whole grains, and fruits. These foods not only replace the nutrients lost by eliminating their white counterparts but also provide an abundance of vitamins, minerals, and antioxidants that can enhance your health in ways you might not have imagined.

Now that you've equipped yourself with the knowledge and tools to make these changes, it's time to put them into action. Remember, every meal is an opportunity to nourish your body and make choices that support your health goals. Don't be discouraged by setbacks or occasional indulgences. What matters most is your overall commitment to eating well and taking care of your body.

Change, especially when it comes to diet, can be challenging, but you're not alone on this journey. Surround yourself with a supportive community—friends, family, or online groups—who share your goals and can offer encouragement, advice, and accountability along the way. Sharing your experiences, challenges, and successes with others can make the process more enjoyable and less daunting.

Be patient with yourself as you adapt to this new way of eating. It takes time for changes to become habits, and it's okay to take small steps. Celebrate your progress, no matter how incremental it may seem. Each healthy choice is a victory worth acknowledging.

Lastly, remember that the "Eat Nothing White" diet is not about deprivation but rather about making mindful, informed food choices that enhance your life. It's a sustainable approach to eating that encourages you to explore a variety of foods, discover new flavors, and enjoy the benefits of a balanced, nutritious diet.

Thank you for investing the time to read through this guide and for taking steps toward a healthier you. Your dedication to learning and improving your health is truly commendable. Keep pushing forward, stay curious, and never underestimate your ability to make positive changes in your life. Here's to a future abundant with flavorful, healthful meals that nurture your physical well-being and your spirit. You possess the capability to make this happen, and the most promising outcomes lie ahead.

FAQs

What exactly is the "Eat Nothing White" diet?

The "Eat Nothing White" diet focuses on eliminating white foods from your diet, particularly those high in processed sugars and refined flour, such as white bread, pasta, rice, and sugar. The principle behind this diet is that these foods can lead to blood sugar spikes, weight gain, and other health issues. Instead, this diet encourages the consumption of whole grains, proteins, fruits, and vegetables.

Can I eat white vegetables and fruits on this diet?

Yes, white vegetables and fruits, such as cauliflower, garlic, onions, potatoes (in moderation), bananas, and pears, are allowed and encouraged on the "Eat Nothing White" diet. These foods are naturally occurring and are packed with essential nutrients beneficial for your health.

Is the "Eat Nothing White" diet suitable for everyone?

While the "Eat Nothing White" diet can be beneficial for many, it's always best to consult with a healthcare provider or a nutritionist before starting any new diet plan, especially for individuals with specific health conditions or dietary needs.

How does the "Eat Nothing White" diet benefit my health?

By reducing the intake of white foods, particularly those with refined sugars and flour, you may experience several health benefits such as improved blood sugar control, reduced risk of heart disease, better digestive health, and potential weight loss. This diet also encourages the consumption of a variety of nutrient-dense foods which can overall improve your health.

Will I need to permanently eliminate white foods from my diet?

The "Eat Nothing White" diet is more about awareness and moderation rather than strict elimination forever. It teaches you to make healthier food choices and understand the impact of certain foods on your body. Over time, you might reintroduce some white foods in moderation, focusing on maintaining a balanced and nutritious diet.

Are there any risks associated with the "Eat Nothing White" diet?

For most people, the "Eat Nothing White" diet is safe and can lead to a healthier eating pattern. However, it's important not to exclude the necessary nutrients your body needs. Ensuring a well-rounded diet that includes a wide range of vitamins and minerals is crucial. Always consult with a healthcare professional to ensure this diet is right for you.

Pantry

Begin by gradually reducing the amount of white foods in your diet, such as replacing white bread with whole grain alternatives, choosing brown rice over white rice, and opting for natural sweeteners like honey or maple syrup instead of white sugar. Focus on incorporating a variety of colors and nutrients into your meals to ensure a balanced diet.

References and Helpful Links

TIMESOFINDIA.COM. (2020, February 16). What is no-white diet for weight loss? Does it really work? The Times of India.
https://timesofindia.indiatimes.com/life-style/health-fitness/diet/what-is-no-white-diet-for-weight-loss-does-it-really-work/articleshow/74159238.cms

Eat Nothing White Diet: A Beginner's Step-by-Step Guide with Recipes and a Meal Plan: Spellmann, Tyler: 9781656763433: Amazon.com: Books. (n.d.).
https://www.amazon.com/Nothing-White-Diet-Step-Step/dp/1656763435

Claudia. (2022, April 12). White Foods: Should you Avoid a White Diet? (Myth or Fact). DarioHealth.
https://www.dariohealth.com/blog/dont-eat-anything-whitereally/

How much sugar is too much? (2023, May 10). www.heart.org.
https://www.heart.org/en/healthy-living/healthy-eating/eat-smart/sugar/how-much-sugar-is-too-much

Glastetter, T., & Glastetter, T. (2018, March 15). Eat Nothing White Diet | The Daily Nexus. The Daily Nexus | the University of California, Santa Barbara's Independent, Student-run Newspaper.
https://dailynexus.com/2018-03-19/eat-nothing-white-diet/#:~:text=The%20diet%20calls%20for%20you,like%20butter%20and%20cheddar%20cheese.

Ld, A. H. R. (2020, January 21). 7 White foods — and what to eat instead. Healthline. https://www.healthline.com/nutrition/white-foods

10 best No white Diet Recipes | Yummly. (n.d.). Yummly. https://www.yummly.com/recipes/no-white-diet

No white diet. (n.d.). Pinterest. https://www.pinterest.com/genevievebryant/no-white-diet/

Carbs by Color | Nutrition. (n.d.). Division of Diabetes Treatment and Prevention. https://www.ihs.gov/diabetes/education-materials-and-resources/diabetes-topics/nutrition/carbs-by-color/#:~:text=White%20Carbs&text=Processed%20grains%20and%20sugar%20are,fry%20bread%2C%20and%20instant%20noodles.

www.ingramcontent.com/pod-product-compliance
Lightning Source LLC
LaVergne TN
LVHW012034060526
838201LV00061B/4602